THE CARDBOARD BOX BOOK

D1541812

Hi, I'm Boxy!

Yeah!

Written by Sarah Powell
Illustrated and designed by Barbi Sido
Crafts designed and made by Bethany Side
Photography by Dan Pangbourne

The crafts in this book should be
supervised by a grown-up.

Copyright © 2014 St. Martin's Press, LLC
175 Fifth Avenue, New York, NY 10010

Created for St. Martin's Press by priddy☺books

All rights reserved, including the right of
reproduction in whole or in part in any form.

1 2 3 4 5 6 7 8 9 10

Manufactured in China April 2014

WHAT'S INSIDE?

BEEP!
BEEP!

MEET BOXY!

I may be a little bit square, but I'm definitely not boring! Cardboard is awesome.

This book will help you recycle cardboard to make some cool, fun, and incredible things to play with that all begin with just one box!

Look out for my crafting tips throughout the book.

To begin, you'll need some basic equipment....

BASIC CRAFTING EQUIPMENT LIST

- GLUE
- PAINTBRUSH
- APRON
- PENCIL
- RULER
- SCISSORS, OR A SCALPEL AND CUTTING BOARD

On each craft, the blue flash tells you the main box you will need.

Small delivery box

SPECIAL EQUIPMENT

Most of the crafts can be made using things you have at home, but there are some special pieces of equipment that you might want to use. These can be found in stationery shops, online, or in specialist craft outlets.

1 **Scalpel and cutting board**
When scissors won't do the trick, use these to cut through thick cardboard. Only grown-ups should use them.

2 **Large hole punch**
Useful for making lots and lots of circles quickly.

3 **Compass**
Handy for drawing circles in the exact size you need.

4 **Metallic paints**
Make your craft look extra-special!

5 **Patterned ribbon**
Great for covering and hiding edges.

6 **Split pins**
Make parts of your crafts movable.

7 **Washi tape**
Super-cool patterned tape.

8 **Decorations, such as stick-on gems**
Add that finishing touch.

9 **Colored card stock**
Add splashes of color to your cardboard boxes.

10 **White pen**
Great for adding details and patterns.

Make your crafts extra-cool!

5

GINGERBREAD HOUSE

Small delivery box

What you will need:

- Small cardboard box
- Large hole punch or jar lid
- Decorations (gems and buttons)
- Paper straws
- Craft templates
- White pen
- White and brown card stock
- Double-sided tape
- Colored card stock

1

Take the cardboard box. Using a pencil, draw the roof and a sidewall on opposite sides.

Using a white pen, draw a circular pattern along the corners (A) and base. Leave a gap for the door at the front.

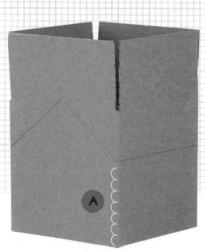

A

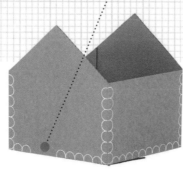

Cut out the roof and sidewalls.

2

Make the roof cover. Use a piece of white card stock that is larger than the box.

Guidelines for the roof

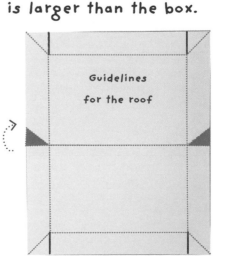

First, mark up the card stock to match the guideline

Fold along the orange dotted lines. Cut along the black lines, and cut out the orange triangles.

Now fold the card stock and glue in place.

3 For the icing, draw a wavy line onto strips of white card stock (B) and cut out (C). Add the icing to the roof cover once it has been decorated.

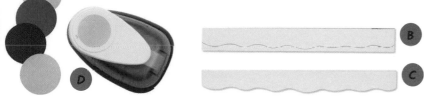

To decorate the roof, use a large hole punch (D) or jar lid to make colored circles.

Start from the bottom and use double-sided tape to stick the circles onto the roof in a repeat pattern. For edges use semicircles (E).

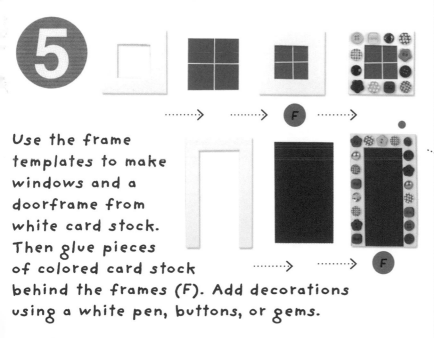

4 To decorate the edges of the house, glue two straws onto each corner and then a third straw on top of these. When dry, cut the straws to match the height of the box.

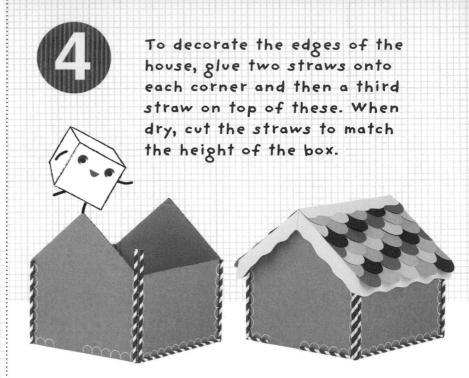

Decorate the base edges by gluing one straw along each side. Trim the straws to fit. Leave a gap for the door. Put the roof on!

5 Use the frame templates to make windows and a doorframe from white card stock. Then glue pieces of colored card stock behind the frames (F). Add decorations using a white pen, buttons, or gems.

You can make a little gingerbread man using the template, brown card stock, gems, and a white pen.

Add details to your house such as white dots and more gems!

Finished!

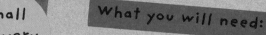

Small delivery box

What you will need:

- Flattened cardboard box
- Thick cardboard tube
- Compass
- Ribbon
- Paint (we used turquoise)
- Pretty patterned paper
- Small ball

Let's get crafting!

1

Make the large cake plates by drawing two circles onto cardboard measuring 9 inches and 6 inches in diameter. Cut these out.

TIP: Use a compass and pencil to draw the circles.

Next, place the cardboard tube in the center of each plate (A). Draw around it, then cut out the holes you have drawn (B).

TIP: Cut inside the lines you have drawn by $\frac{1}{32}$ inch to ensure a tight fit.

2

Draw and cut out three smaller circles, two measuring 3 inches and one measuring 2 inches in diameter.

As in step 1, place the cardboard tube in the center of each circle. Draw around it and cut out the holes.

3

Paint the cardboard tube, ball, three small circles, and two large plates in a pretty color. Leave to dry.

Put your apron on, too!

4

To decorate your plates, draw and cut out two circles (around 7 inches and 5 inches in diameter) from the pretty paper (C).

Glue the paper onto the plates. Cut out the centers (D).

Take the ribbon (E) and wrap it around the edge of each plate and the three smaller circles. Cut, then glue into place.

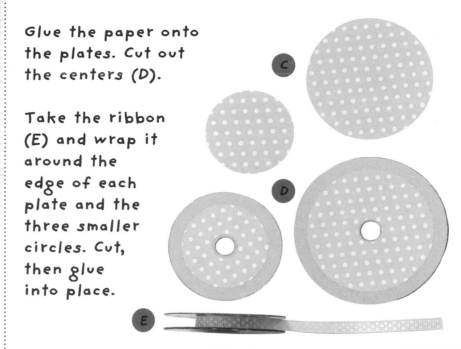

5

Using the picture below to help you, assemble your stand by sliding the circles and plates onto the tube.

TIP: Make sure you assemble them in order, starting with the smallest circle first.

Glue the ball onto the top of the tube (F).

Looks great!

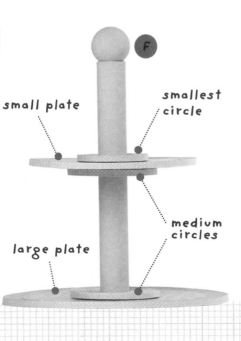

small plate

smallest circle

medium circles

large plate

Finished!

Decorate with toys or real cakes!

Mmm, cake!

9

BOX FRIENDS

Small square box

What you will need:

- Small cardboard box
- Extra sheets of cardboard
- Cardboard tube for legs
- Craft templates
- Black card stock
- Yogurt cup for hat
- Googly eyes
- Tape
- Black paint
- Black pen
- Two split pins
- Compass

1

Use the arm, nose, and foot templates to make two arms, two feet, and two noses from cardboard.

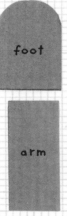

foot   foot   2 noses

nose

foot

arm

(3 inches)

A

Draw and cut out a circular hat base from cardboard (A).

TIP: Use your compass to draw the hat base.

2

Make the glasses and mustache from black card stock using the templates (B).

C

D

B

Cut the cardboard tube in half to make two legs. Place the legs on top of the feet and draw around the base of each leg (C). Cut out the holes (D).

3

Draw around the circular base of the yogurt cup (E) onto the hat base from step 1. Cut out the circle.

Push the yogurt cup through hole (F), then paint it black (G).

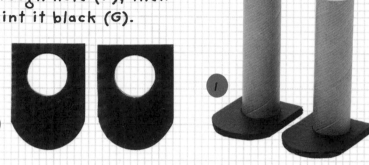

Paint the feet black (H). Once dry, fit the legs into the feet (I).

4

Take the small box, and glue the legs to the base (J).

On each arm, make a light fold as shown.

Fix the arms to the box using split pins (K).

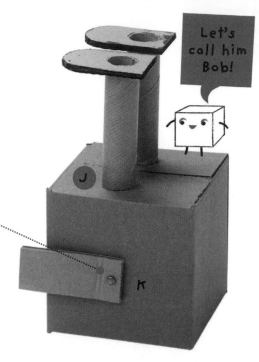

Let's call him Bob!

TIP: It helps if the top of the box is open when attaching the arms to the sides.

5

Glue on the hat. Glue on the mustache followed by the first nose, glasses, and second nose.

Glue on the eyes and draw on a smile with the black pen.

Finished!

Hello!

11

CARDBOARD CITY

Food packaging boxes

What you will need:

- Large piece of cardboard for play mat
- Extra sheets of cardboard
- Lots of used box packaging for buildings
- Gray card stock
- Craft templates
- Brown paper
- Tape
- Washi tape
- White pen
- Black pen

Be careful!

1 Plan your road layout on the large piece of cardboard and cut out strips of gray card stock to match.

Hand drawn road markings

Washi tape

Draw on road markings using a white pen. Stick down the gray strips onto the cardboard with glue, then line the roads with washi tape.

2 To make the buildings, begin by placing your box packaging around the roads.

When the boxes are in the positions you want, take each box in turn and wrap it in brown paper.

3

To wrap up a box, cut the brown paper so it is big enough to wrap around the box (A).

Tape the edges down along the back (B).

Use your tape!

A

B

C

At each end, fold in a long edge, then fold the two shorter edges (C). Fold the remaining long edge and tape in place.

4

With a black pen, draw on windows and doors.

When you've finished, glue the base of each building to the city layout.

5

To make building signs, cut the end off a piece of cardboard, then cut this end diagonally in half.

These triangles are stands for your sign. Glue these onto the back of the sign (D). Decorate using the templates.

Be careful!

D

E

F

The roofs are made in a similar way, however, to make the stands, you should cut off the corners (E). Use a black pen to decorate (F).

HOSPITAL

School

LIBRARY

CAFÉ

M·A·R·K·E·T

FIRE STATION

STOP

Finished!

Place the signs and roofs on the buildings. Now it's playtime!

PLAYHOUSE

What you will need:

Extra-large box

- Extra-large cardboard box
- Extra sheets of cardboard
- Small box for chimney
- Cylindrical packaging or cardboard tube
- Different-colored sheets of card stock or paper
- Masking tape
- Small box for doghouse
- Paint: white, blue, and black
- Craft templates
- Jar lid

 Take the large cardboard box. On opposite sides, use a pencil to draw the roof and sidewalls.

Cut these out.

This can be tricky!

2 On the two long sides, draw two windows.

Cut out the four squares within each window frame.

Paint the frames white and leave to dry.

TIP: For an easier version, simply paint windows onto the box.

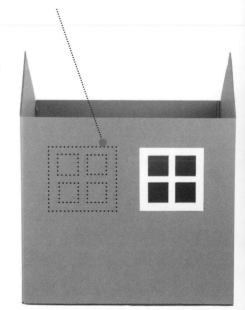

14

3

Draw a door on one side of the box. Add the window design from step 2 and cut out the four frame squares.

Next, cut out the door, along the top, right-hand side, and base.

TIP: Score inside the door with a cutting tool to help the door open and close.

Paint the door blue and leave to dry.

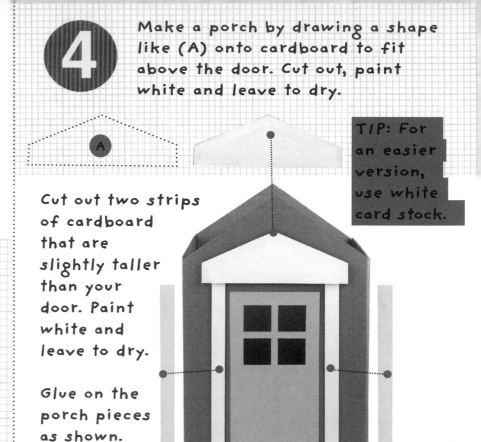

4

Make a porch by drawing a shape like (A) onto cardboard to fit above the door. Cut out, paint white and leave to dry.

Ⓐ

TIP: For an easier version, use white card stock.

Cut out two strips of cardboard that are slightly taller than your door. Paint white and leave to dry.

Glue on the porch pieces as shown.

5

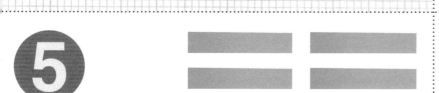

Cut out windowsills from cardboard and paint blue. Once dry, stick under each window with glue.

TIP: For an easier version, use blue card stock.

It's taking shape!

6

Make the roof cover from two large sheets of cardboard.

Attach together with masking tape.

15

7

Tile your roof using lots of square colored pieces of card stock or paper. Glue the "tiles" on. Start from the bottom and work your way to the top.

When you reach an end, you may need to trim the tiles to fit.

TIP: For an easier version, you could leave the roof blank, or draw on your own tiles.

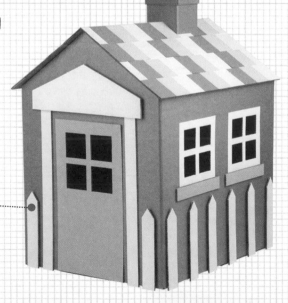

8

Hold the chimney box against the top of the roof. Mark the angle made by the roof onto the chimney and cut out.

Glue strips of cardboard around the top of the chimney as shown.

Cut the cylindrical container or cardboard tube to size. Paint black. Glue onto the box. Put the chimney on the roof.

9

Make the white picket fence by drawing and cutting out posts from cardboard (we made 20). Paint white and leave to dry.

Position the posts around the house, then glue them on.

10

Next, cut out long strips of white card stock and glue to the posts as shown.

Add a grass border around the base by drawing a grass shape onto green card stock. Cut this out and glue onto the fence.

11

Make a "WELCOME" mat by cutting out the templates and gluing onto bright card stock.

Cut out the keyhole template and glue onto the door.

Make a door handle from two small cardboard circles, one smaller than the other (B). Draw around jar lids, cut out, and glue together. Paint white, leave to dry. Glue onto the door.

12

Make the doghouse by drawing a roof and sidewalls on the small box. Draw a door, too.

Use a piece of bright card stock for the roof. Simply fold in half and place on top.

Cut out the roof, sidewalls, and door. Glue the "DEXTER" template to the front.

Finished!

Check out my house!

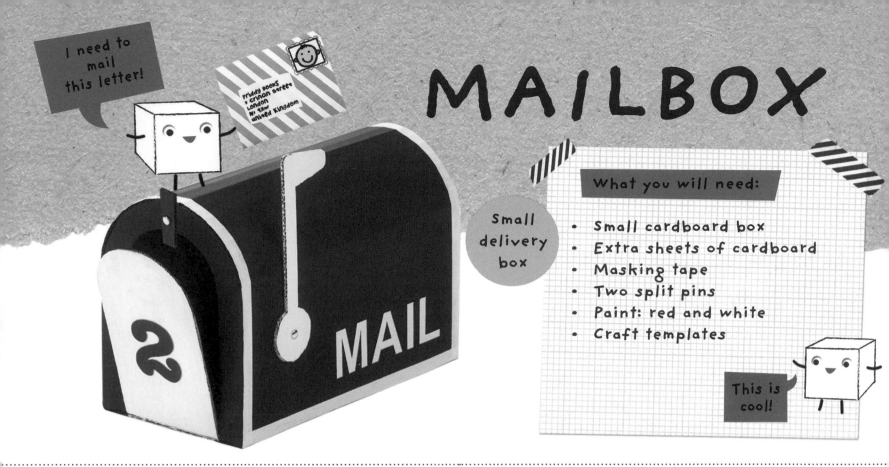

MAILBOX

What you will need:

- Small cardboard box
- Extra sheets of cardboard
- Masking tape
- Two split pins
- Paint: red and white
- Craft templates

Small delivery box

This is cool!

1

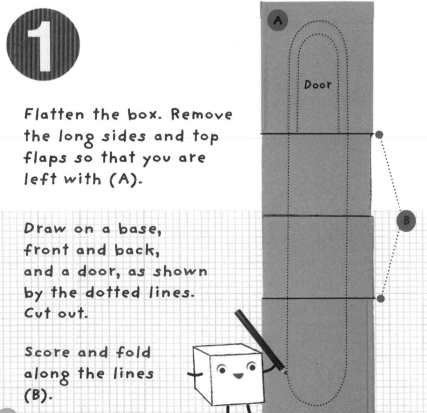

Flatten the box. Remove the long sides and top flaps so that you are left with (A).

Draw on a base, front and back, and a door, as shown by the dotted lines. Cut out.

Score and fold along the lines (B).

Door

2

Make supports from four strips of cardboard (C). Fold and glue each strip to form (D). Glue the supports to the four corners of the base of the mailbox.

When dry, glue the front and back of the mailbox to the supports (E).

Stick here!

3 Make the roof by wrapping a long piece of cardboard around the mailbox base.

Firstly, use masking tape to stick the cardboard to one side of the base (F). Roll the cardboard around the mailbox to form the roof (G).

Tape down the roof with masking tape. Cut off excess cardboard (H).

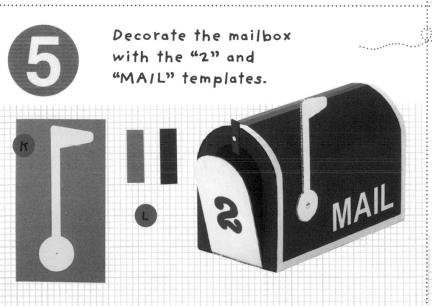

TIP: When rolling the roof, roll with the grain of the cardboard.

4 Paint the door white, and the rest of the mailbox red. Leave to dry.

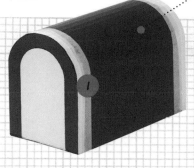
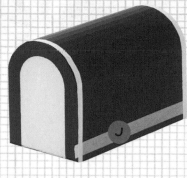

Use masking tape to make a border (I) around the front and back of the mailbox. Paint the borders white. Leave to dry before removing the tape.

Repeat this step to make the two base borders along the long edges of the mailbox (J).

5 Decorate the mailbox with the "2" and "MAIL" templates.

Make the flag from cardboard using the template (K). Paint white, then attach to the mailbox with a split pin. Make a door latch from a small piece of cardboard (L). Paint red, then attach using a split pin.

Finished!

Posted!

Priddy BOOKS
+ crinan street
London
N1 9Xw
united Kingdom

How many letters will you receive in your mailbox?

GIANT DICE

Medium square box

What you will need:

- Square cardboard box
- Extra sheets of cardboard
- Six different-colored paints
- Small jar lid
- White card stock
- Washi tape

1 To make a dice, take your box and trace around it twice on cardboard. Cut these squares out.

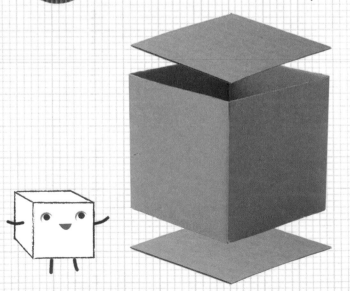

Cut the flaps off the top and bottom of the box so that you are left with four sides.

2 Paint each side with different-colored paints and leave to dry.

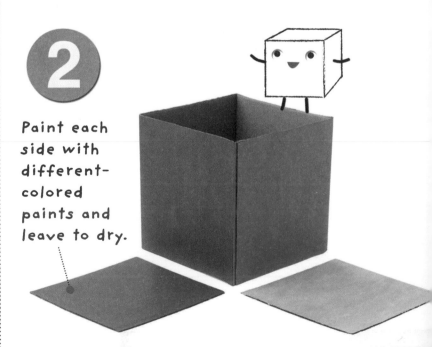

TIP: Don't worry about painting to a neat edge as these will be covered with washi tape.

3

Use washi tape to stick the squares to the top and bottom.

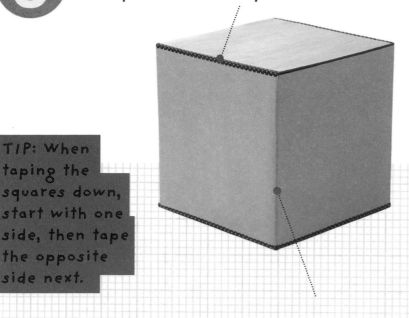

TIP: When taping the squares down, start with one side, then tape the opposite side next.

Tape down each corner edge of the box, so every side is lined with washi tape.

4

Make the dice spots using a small jar lid to draw 21 circles on white card stock. Cut out.

Now it's time to position the spots! Start with a number and side of your choice and glue on the spots.

TIP: To position the spots perfectly, cut out two strips of paper of the same width (A) and (B). Use these as positioning tools so that the corner spots are always in the same place on all sides.

5

Use the layouts below to help you position the spots.

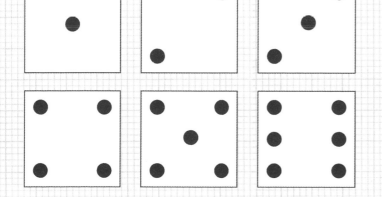

Remember that each opposite side should add up to 7; for example, 6 and 1 should be on opposite sides of the dice.

Finished!

Play your favorite board game!

Throw it!

HAY BARN

Small delivery box

What you will need:

- Small cardboard delivery box
- Extra sheets of cardboard
- Masking tape
- Paint: red and white
- Black card stock
- Double-sided tape

1

Carefully cut the top flaps into a barn roof shape, as shown.

Tape the flaps together using masking tape.

A

Cool!

Cut out an extra piece of cardboard to cover the hole at the top of the barn. Tape in place (A).

2

Draw a door on the front and draw a window on the side of the box.

Cut out the door and window. Make sure you leave one side of the door uncut.

3

Paint the barn red, leaving the roof unpainted.

TIP: You will need to give it 3–4 coats to get a really rich red color.

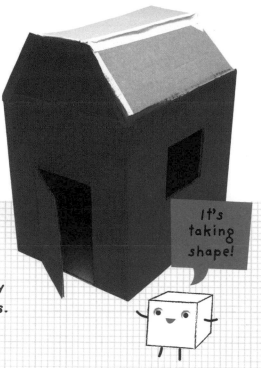

It's taking shape!

Let the paint dry in between coats.

4

Use masking tape to create an "X" on the door and a border under the roof, around the door and around the window.

Paint each taped-off area and border white, coating 3–4 times.

Once the paint is dry, carefully remove the tape.

5

Measure the area of the roof, and draw this onto black card stock.

Cut out the roof from the black card stock. Use double-sided tape to stick the roof onto the barn.

Finished!

PLAY OVEN

Extra-large box

What's cooking?

What you will need:

- Extra-large cardboard box
- Extra cardboard for details and accessories
- Compass
- Masking tape
- Double-sided tape
- Brown tape
- Paint: silver and white
- White and gray card stock
- Split pin
- Plastic sheet protector
- Craft templates

1

Take your box, lay it down on its side, and open the flaps out as shown.

Cool!

On the front, using a pencil and ruler, draw a square, just like the black dotted line shown in the picture above.

2

Within that square, draw a control panel and the main oven door area.

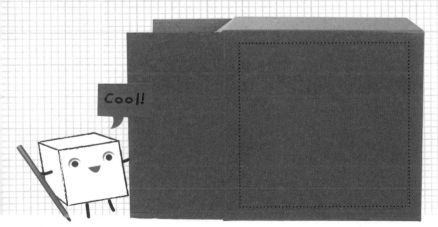

Control panel

Main oven door

3 Next, draw a rectangle for the oven door window. Carefully cut this out.

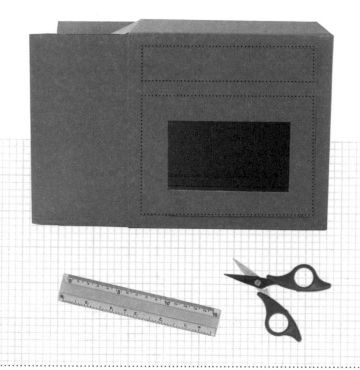

4 Cut along three sides of the oven door, leaving one side uncut (A).

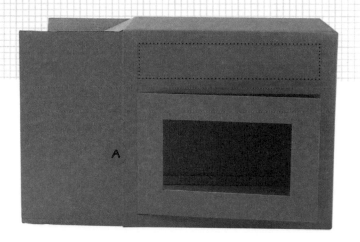

Score a line along the uncut side from the inside of the box. This will help the door to open and close.

5 Use masking tape to make a border (B) around the window and two lines at opposite sides of the door (C). Paint the taped-off areas white.

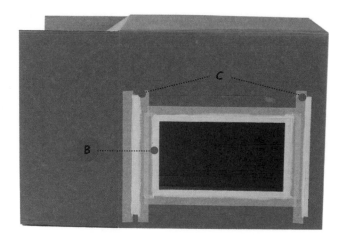

Leave to dry, then remove the tape. Use brown tape to close the side flaps.

6 To make oven shelf ledges, cut out two long strips of cardboard (D). Use double-sided tape to stick each one to the inside of the oven.

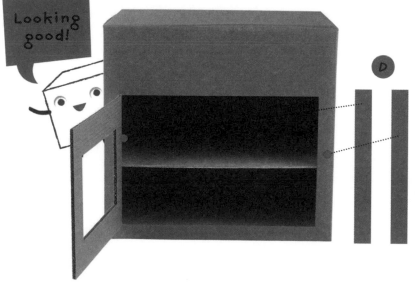

Looking good!

Make a cardboard shelf that matches the interior, then place on top of the ledges.

7

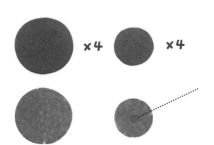

Cut out a piece of cardboard to match the control panel area and paint white. Leave to dry.

For the controls, cut out four larger circles and four smaller ones.

x4 x4

Paint silver and leave to dry. Glue the smaller circles onto the larger ones, then glue these onto the control panel.

8

E
F

To make the oven stove, cut out four rings (E) and four circles (F) from cardboard. Paint silver. Leave to dry.

Cut out four circles from gray card stock, the same size as the rings. Glue together as shown.

TIP: For a simpler version, simply paint four cardboard circles to look like oven rings

+

9

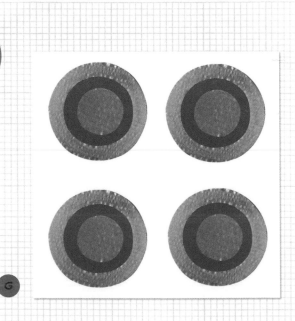

G

Glue the oven rings onto a piece of white card stock (G) that fits the oven top, then glue this onto the oven top. Glue the control panel to the front of the oven.

10

H

I

Cut out a back panel from cardboard. Paint this white. Leave to dry, then glue to the oven back.

Cut out the clockface template. Glue onto a cardboard circle (H).

Use the clock hand templates to make clock hands from gray card stock. Attach to the clock with a split pin (I). Glue the clock to the back panel (J).

J

11 To make a handle, stick two strips of cardboard together, paint silver (K), then leave to dry. Glue onto the oven door.

To make a hook for utensils, glue together two small cardboard squares (L), paint silver, leave to dry, then glue to the back panel. Repeat to make another.

Door handle K

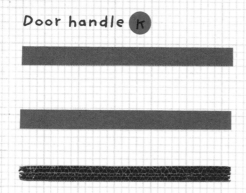

You're nearly done!

Utensil hook L

12

Using double-sided tape, attach a plastic sheet protector to the inside of the oven door to look like glass.

Hang up your utensils, put on your chef hat, and get cooking!

Let's bake cookies!

Finished!

FAIRY WINGS

What you will need:

- Cereal box
- Pink pearlized paint
- White and pink paper
- Double-sided tape
- Pretty patterned card stock
- Decorative stickers
- Ribbon
- Small jar lid

Cereal box

Fairy power!

1 Flatten a cereal box. Draw a wing on one half and cut out (A). Use the cutout as a template to draw the other wing (B).

A

B

TIP: Remember, you will need to turn over the cutout before drawing the second wing!

2 Trim the middle section, removing the excess cardboard as shown.

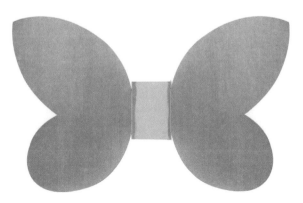

Paint your wings in the color of your choice. Boxy used a pretty pearlized pink. Leave the paint to dry.

3

Take a large piece of white paper, fold in half, and draw on wing segments (C). Cut out and glue onto each of the wings (D).

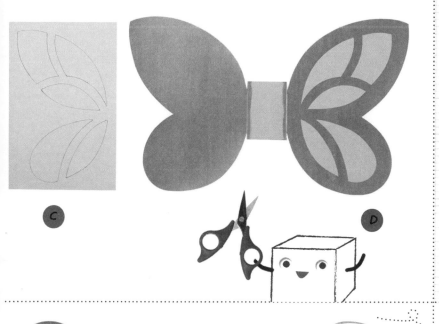

C

D

4

Over the middle section, stick two strips of double-sided tape, then place two long pieces of ribbon on the tape.

Cut out a circle from patterned card stock (E) and glue to the center of the wings (F), over the ribbon.

E

F

5

Use a small jar lid to draw and cut out five small circles from white paper and one out of pink paper (G).

Stick these onto the central circle to make a flower. Decorate with pretty stickers.

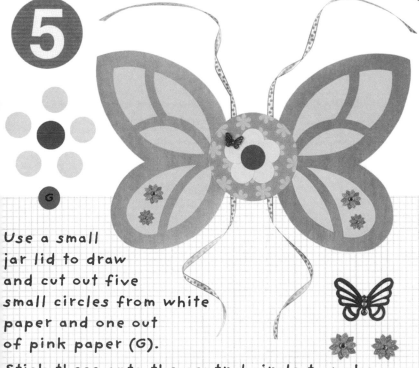

G

Finished!

Tie the ribbons around the front of your body and flutter like a fairy!

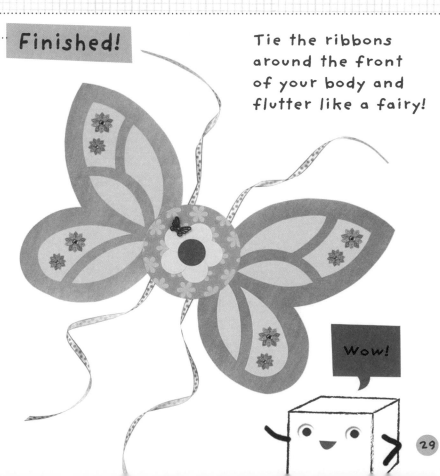

Wow!

ROCKIN' ROBOT

Small/
medium
boxes

What you will need:

- Small square cardboard box
- Medium-sized cardboard box
- Extra sheets of cardboard
- Craft templates
- Different-colored paints
- Two yogurt cups
- Aluminium foil
- Compass
- Bottle lids
- Two chenille stems
- Two pom-poms
- Chunky pen

1

For the head, remove the flaps on one end of the small box, leaving a small lip of cardboard on each side (A).

TIP: Trim the corners off each lip so they will not overlap when glued down.

A

For the body, take the larger box and remove the flaps on one end.

2

Place the eye templates on the head. Trace around the eyeholes with a pencil and cut out.

Make a hole for your head on the body box.

TIP: Measure the size of your head first, then use a compass.

Next, draw and cut out holes for your arms to fit through.

3 Stick the head to the top of the body box (B). Paint blue and leave to dry.

Glue on the eyes and mouth templates. Next stick on two yogurt cups to make ears (C).

4 Design a control panel using cardboard squares, rectangles, and circles (D).

Wrap the circles in aluminium foil to look like bolts.

Paint the control panel and pieces in bright colors. When dry, glue together.

Finish the control panel with the dial templates and bottle lids for buttons.

5 Use a compass to make an antennae base. Draw two cardboard circles. Cut these out. Glue together, then wrap in aluminium foil.

Wrap a chenille stem around a chunky pen and then remove. Stick to the antennae base with tape. Place a pom-pom in the top coil. Repeat.

Finished!

We rock!

TRAIN

What you will need:

- Small food-packaging boxes
- Extra sheets of cardboard
- Different-colored paints
- 14 split pins
- Six treasury tags
- Compass or jar lid
- Ice pop sticks
- Craft templates

Small food boxes

Choo! Choo!

1

Find packaging similar to the picture below that can make a train engine and two cars.

Cut a cardboard tube to make one tall and one small chimney (A).

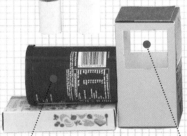

(A)

This is a cylinder!

On the driver's compartment, draw windows on all sides, then cut out.

Cut the tops off both of the cars.

2

Draw and cut out three cardboard bases for the engine and two car boxes to be glued onto. Paint red, leave to dry.

Engine base	Car base	Car base

 × 14

Draw and cut out 14 wheels, paint them black, and leave to dry.

TIP: Use a compass and pencil to draw the circles, or trace around a small jar lid.

3 To attach the wheels, paint a strip of glue to the back of each one and stick to the sides of the bases. Push split pins through the center of each wheel.

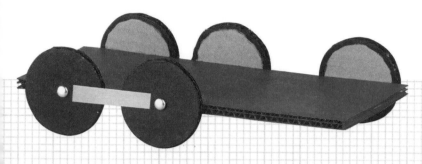

When the glue is dry, cut ice pop sticks to size and glue them between the wheels as shown. You can paint the ice pop sticks if you wish.

4 Cut out a cardboard roof for the driver's compartment and paint in a bright color (B).

Paint each section of the train in different colors. Leave to dry.

Glue the engine together.

5 Stick the train templates to your train.

Glue the engine and the cars to their bases. When dry, attach the engine and the cars together using treasury tags (C).

TIP: Make holes for the treasury tags by pushing a pencil through the boxes.

And we are off!

Finished!

MARKET STAND

Large delivery box

What you will need:

- Large cardboard box
- Cereal box
- Three identical small boxes
- Small square box
- Extra sheets of cardboard
- Card stock: green, white, red, and black
- Paint: white, green, and red
- String
- Patterned ribbon
- Double-sided tape
- Chalk

Got my list!

1 To make the stand, paint the front of the large box white. Leave to dry.

Let's go!

Then glue a piece of green card stock to the top of it.

2 Make flags by cutting out four diamonds from red card stock. Fold each diamond in half.

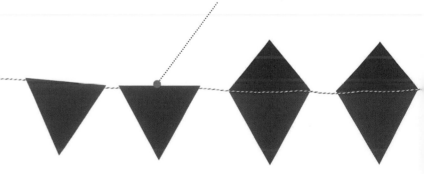

Lay out the string, evenly spacing the flags along it. Fold the flags around the string and glue together.

3

Take two large pieces of cardboard that are the same width as the large box but twice the height.

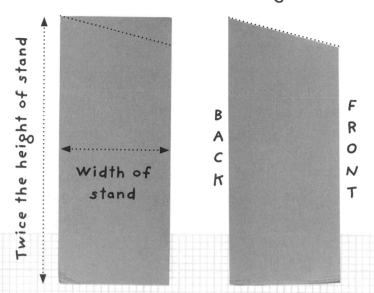

Twice the height of stand

Width of stand

BACK

FRONT

At the tops, mark a diagonal line, then cut the tops off both. These will be the side panels.

4

Tape the flag string to the sides of the stand.

Stick the side panels to the stand using double-sided tape.

Glue patterned ribbon down the front edge of the side panels (A).

5

Make the roof from a large piece of cardboard.

Glue the roof onto the top of the side panels as shown.

6

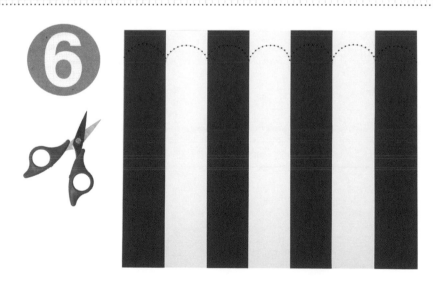

Make the roof canopy from red card stock. It needs to be slightly longer than the roof. Glue three long strips of white card stock onto the red card stock, then draw a wavy edge on one end, as shown by the dotted line.

7

Once the glue has dried, cut out the wavy edge.

Glue the canopy to the roof. Fold down down the overhang.

8

To make a shelf for the front of the stand, cut down a cereal box as shown (B).

Then cut one long side, so only a strip remains (C).

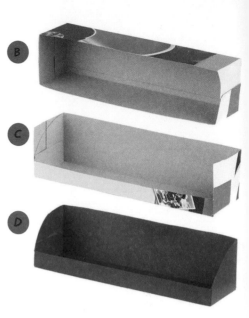

Draw curves on either side and cut out. Paint it green (D). Leave to dry.

9

Make display shelves using three identical boxes. Cut off their lids, then on one of them, cut off one long side. On the two shorter sides, draw curved lines (E) and cut out.

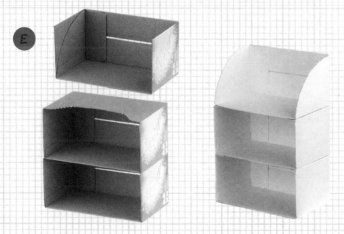

Glue the three boxes together. Paint white and leave to dry.

10

To make a sign, draw and cut out a frame from cardboard.

Paint red and leave to dry.

Cut out a piece of black card stock and stick this to the back of the frame using double-sided tape.

Use chalk to write a message on the sign.

STRAWBERRIES FOR SALE

11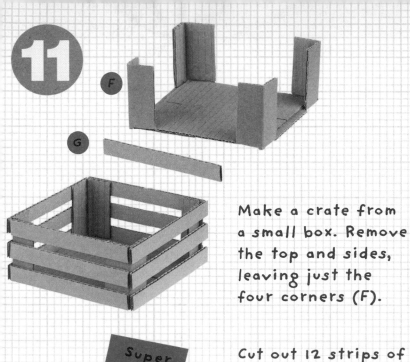

Make a crate from a small box. Remove the top and sides, leaving just the four corners (F).

Cut out 12 strips of cardboard (G) and attach three strips to each side.

Super cool!

You are now open for business!

12 Finally, stick the sign and green shelf to the stand using glue. Leave to dry.

Gather together the things that you are going to sell. Arrange them around the stand, in the crates, and on the shelves.

STRAWBERRIES FOR SALE

Finished!

Great show!

NOW PLAYING
Once Upon a Time
SHOW TIMES
Every day at 2 p.m. and 6 p.m.

Small tissue boxes

What you will need:

- Two identical tissue boxes
- Paint: white and yellow
- Double-sided tape or fabric glue
- Paper: orange, green, blue, and yellow
- Felt: green and yellow
- Red ribbon
- Two bendable straws
- Craft templates
- Ice pop sticks
- Red card stock

1 To make the stage, on one tissue box draw a rectangle. Cut it out (A).

Draw another rectangle on top of the box, and cut out (B). Paint yellow and leave to dry.

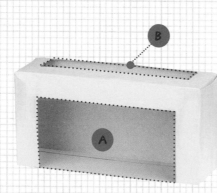

Paint the second tissue box white. Leave to dry.

2 Make scenery for the stage. Draw and cut out two hills (C), and grass (D) from paper. Layer over a piece of blue paper (E). Glue together.

Finally, draw and cut out a piece of green paper to fit the stage floor area (F).

D

E

3

Open one of the sides of the yellow box and glue the scenery and floor to the inside. Glue the box sides back together.

Create a striped pattern on the white box using strips of orange paper.

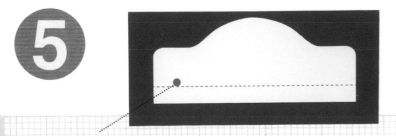

Glue the boxes together, then cover the join using ribbon.

4

Make stage curtains from two rectangles of green felt.

Fold the top of one piece of felt over a straw. Stick down with double-sided tape or fabric glue (G).

G

Push the felt along the straw toward the bend. Fold the straw end over and tape down (H). Repeat.

H

Cut out two strips of yellow felt and tie around the middle (I) of each curtain. Use tape to stick the curtains onto the stage.

I

5

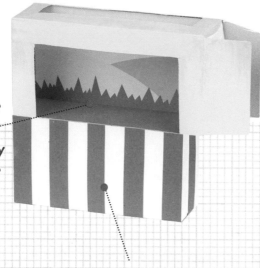

Make the sign from red card stock using the template. Fold along the dashed line.

Glue the sign to the top of the theater.

Cut out the "Now playing" sign and glue to the bottom of the theater.

Finished!

Make puppets by sticking characters onto ice pop sticks!

Time for the show!

Pretty!

PRINCESS CASTLE

What you will need:

- Small cardboard box
- Five cardboard tubes
- Extra sheets of cardboard
- Two small square tissue boxes
- Pretty paint colors
- Pretty paper
- White pen
- Ribbon
- White paper
- Flower stickers
- Craft templates
- Masking tape

Small square box

1 Take the small box, flatten it, and remove the top flaps. Trim two strips off each side (see dotted line).

Use the small door template to cut out a drawbridge (A). Do not cut along the base.

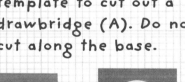

On a piece of cardboard, draw around the large door template and cut out (B). Glue to (A).

Draw and cut out the square edging along the top of each side.

2 Tape a cardboard tube to each of the four corners of the castle using masking tape.

TIP: Tape both the inside and outside!

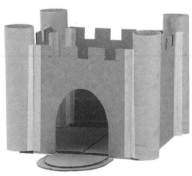

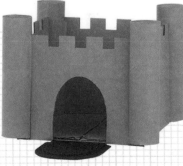

Paint the castle and the fifth tube purple. Paint the drawbridge a darker purple. Leave to dry.

3

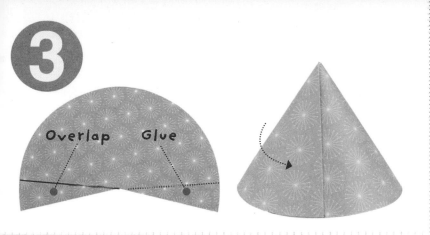

Overlap   Glue

Make roofs for the castle towers using pretty paper and the roof template.

Pretty paper!

Wrap the paper around to form a cone and glue the edges together.

Repeat to make five roofs.

4

Make the central tower by wrapping one tissue box in pretty paper.

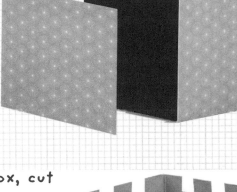

On the second box, cut off the top. Draw and cut out square edging on each side. Paint pink and leave to dry.

Glue the boxes together. Add a strip of pretty paper around the top box for decoration.

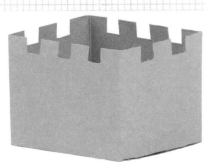

5

Assemble the castle as shown, placing a roof on each tower.

Make the windows from white paper using the templates. Glue on.

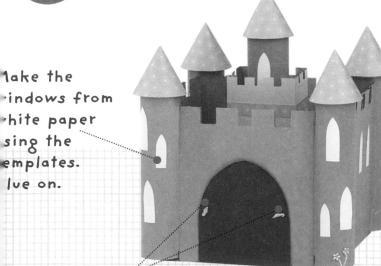

Make two holes in the wall and drawbridge door, thread ribbon through, and tie knots at each end.

Finished!

Decorate by drawing vines and leaves with a white pen. Stick on flower stickers.

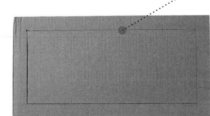

Large delivery box

What you will need:

- Large cardboard box
- Extra sheets of cardboard
- Craft templates
- Paints: red, silver, black, white, orange, and yellow
- Brown tape
- Compass
- Black and gray card stock
- Split pin
- Newspaper

BEEP!
BEEP!

1

Open up the flaps on the top of the large box. Cut off one of the short flaps and save for step 2.

Make the dashboard from the remaining short flap. About 5 inches from the front of the box edge, score a line across the short flap. Bend the scored area downward (A).

The front area will be the hood (B).

2

Make the windshield from the removed short flap. Draw a border inside then cut this out.

Save the removed cardboard to make the grill in steps 5 and 8.

This will be the car windshield.

3

On one of the long flaps near the end of the hood, draw a triangle (C).

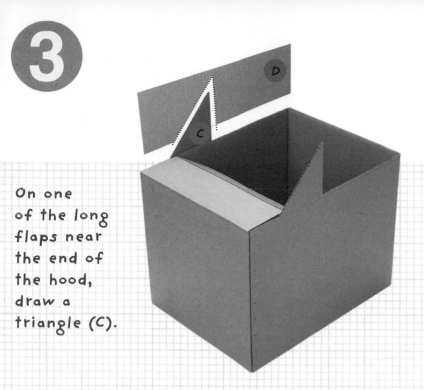

Cut around the triangle to remove the flap. Once removed, use the flap (D) as a template to create the same shape on the opposite side.

4

Use brown tape to stick the hood in place, then attach the windshield to the triangles.

Use your red paint!

When you are happy with your car, paint the outside red and leave to dry.

5

Make four cardboard wheels measuring 8 inches in diameter. Paint them black (E).

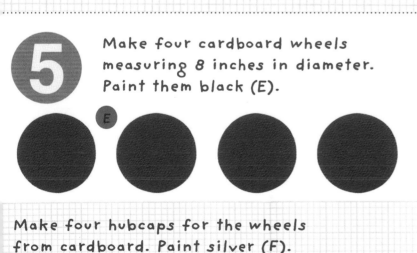

Make four hubcaps for the wheels from cardboard. Paint silver (F).

Glue (E) and (F) together.

TIP: Use a compass and pencil to draw circles.

Paint the cardboard removed in step 2 silver (G).

6

Make four circular cardboard lights measuring 4 inches in diameter. Paint orange (H).

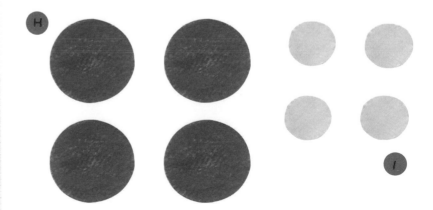

Make four smaller cardboard circles for the inner lights. Paint these yellow (I). Once dry, glue (I) and (H) together.

7

For the license plates, cut out two rectangles from cardboard. Paint these white.

SPEEDY1

From the template sheet cut out "SPEEDY 1" twice, and glue on when the paint is dry.

8

Glue strips of black card stock onto the grill leaving a silver border around the edge, as shown.

Cut out the three dial templates. Set these aside.

Only grown-ups use cutting tools!

9

Make the steering wheel from gray card stock. Draw a wheel shape as shown below.

Cut out sections 1, 2, and 3, and discard.

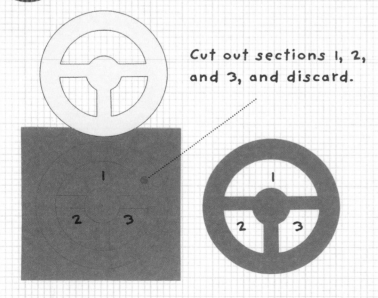

Push the split pin through the center of the steering wheel.

10

Glue the wheels onto the car.

Make the door by cutting a line as shown (J). Inside the car score a line like (K), starting from the windshield down to (J). This helps the door to open and close.

On the front of the car, glue two lights, the grill panel, and one license plate.

On the back of the car, stick on two lights and the second license plate.

12

Paint the dashboard black. Once dry, glue on the dials and attach the steering wheel with the split pin.

TIP: To ensure the sides don't get covered in black paint, place newspaper at each end, as shown.

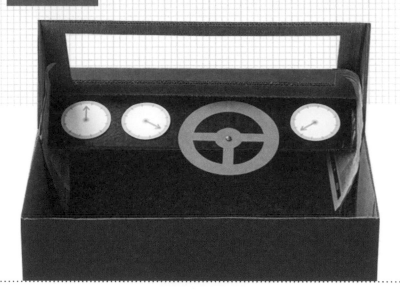

Now it's time get in your car and drive! Where will you go?

Finished!

PLANE

What you will need:

- Large cardboard box
- Medium square-shaped cardboard box
- Extra sheets of cardboard
- Compass or jar lid
- Split pin
- Gray card stock
- Brown tape
- White paper
- White paint
- Craft templates

1 Follow steps 1 to 4 of the car craft (do not paint red). Use the dotted line below as a guide to cut out the sides of the plane.

Make two wings from cardboard. Draw decorations on white paper. Cut out and glue on.

Make horizontal slits on the sides of the plane. Slot in the wings.

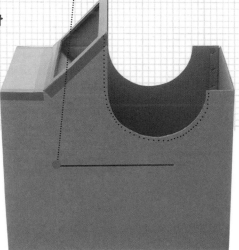

2 Make the tail from cardboard by drawing (A) and (B).

Cut a slit through (A), which is big enough for (B) to fit into.

Decorate the tail with paper circles and stripes. Make a vertical slit on the rear of the plane for the tail to slot through

3

Make the front of the plane from a medium-size box that has been cut down so it is about 8 inches deep. Cut the corners off each flap, ensuring the cuts you make are even.

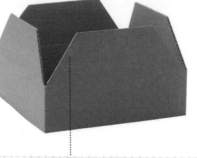

Stick the flaps together with brown tape.

Cover the hole with a square piece of cardboard (C). Tape in place.

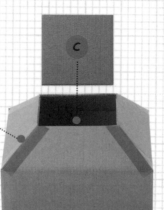

4

Make two cardboard propellers and two circles. One circle should be smaller.

Paint the propellers and the small circle white. Leave to dry.

Attach the box to the front of the plane with brown tape.

Glue on all the propeller pieces, as shown.

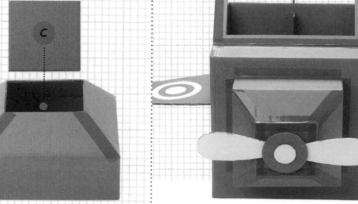

5

Paint the dashboard white. Leave to dry.

Make the wheel by following step 9 from the car craft, but this time cut off the top of the steering wheel, as shown.

Glue the three dial templates to the dashboard.

Finished!   Time to fly!

47

LOOK OUT FOR.....

DELIVERY BOXES

This could make a car.

Flatten this out to make a play mat.

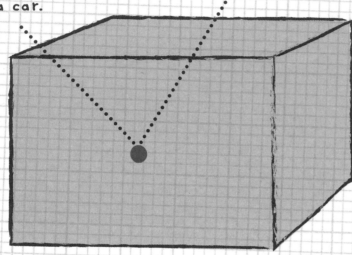

ROLLS AND TUBES

Great for castle towers!

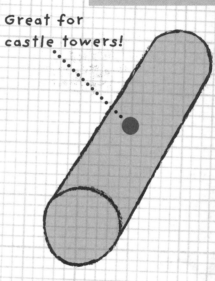

CEREAL BOXES

Transform this into magical fairy wings.

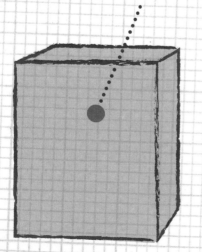

SQUARE BOXES

The perfect shape for a giant dice.

Hey, it's Uncle Pete! HELLO!